REFLECTIVE EDGE

SERIES

For Senior Executives

223 HARD-HITTING
QUESTIONS THAT
WILL TRANSFORM
THE WAY YOU LEAD

DEVIKA DAS

Written by Devika Das

ISBN: 978-988-74252-8-1

Registered at Books Registration Office (Hong Kong)

Printed in Hong Kong

Edited by Claire Severn

Designed by Bay Media Studio

Cover by Saachi Das

Website: www.COREexecutivepresence.com

For my daughters, Saachi and Saisha.
The most courageous thing you can do is
tell yourself the truth. May you always have
the courage to look inward.

CONTENTS

ACKNOWLEDGEMENTS

The Reflective Edge series was crafted while I was in the midst of writing a separate book on executive presence. Provisionally titled *Core Executive Presence for Women*, this required me to research how the deep space within a person changes their outward presence.

After two years of working on the book, I came to the conclusion that self-help as a genre can only be used as guidance because the true meaning of self-help is to look within ourselves for answers. There is so much collective, untapped wisdom within all of us, yet we don't take the time to discover it. We should.

Writing *Reflective Edge: For Senior Executives* has been both an academic and a spiritual endeavour. The questions put me in an uncomfortable position. They challenged me to look at the world as it is and not tinted by the lens I wear to protect myself. No matter who we are in front of the world, once we reflect within to be authentic in our own truth, we become more inclusive in our outlook.

There is no such thing as singular leadership skill; it involves the whole person. You cannot detach yourself in leadership roles. The courage to reflect on yourself translates into accepting not only who you are but also who others are. A conscious leader can impact not only their organization but the wider world as well, and let's face it: the planet is certainly in dire need of some mindful leadership right now.

Of course, I couldn't have written this book alone. To start with, I would like to thank 'the force' that shepherded me through this process. I was in a state of flow that can only be described as some form of 'guidedness,' showing me that there is a lot we can achieve when we are centered. As Anne Lammot would have said: this higher source is a bit of a show off – I'm blessed for it.

Standing on the shoulders of giants: I thank my professors at INSEAD – Manfred Kets de Vries, Erik van de Loo, and especially Roger Lehman, from whom I learnt that if you want to be the force of good, you need to start with yourself. Thank you for giving me the psychological perspective to look within myself and the ability to look deeply into what is 'unseen' in others.

It was at INSEAD that I learned the transformational power of deep, reflective writing. Manfred, who has written several books and is a true leadership guru, once told me that writing helps keeps him sane. I've found that that couldn't be more true. It's wonderful to be able to share the joy of writing with others and help them find sanity themselves.

To my classmates and friends at INSEAD: you have been a constant source of support and encouragement, and for that, I truly thank you.

To Carla Kriwet: thank you for taking the time to look at the first draft of the book and reminding me that some quests would be shorter if I only used Google. Thank you to Nitesh Chaurasia for reflecting on the questions – your feedback was priceless – and to Hendrik Schwartz for generously taking the time to source academic articles from the

INSEAD library when I couldn't travel. To Gautam Bhushan and Mridul Dasgupta: thank you for being the recipients of various versions of covers and ideas in the months preceding the publication of the book.

To Carlos Moncayo: a big thank you for your insight and feedback and for honoring me by taking the time to write the foreword for the book, even at a difficult time. Thanks also to Saachi Das for her design contribution to the cover and to Claire Severn for polishing my words and making them flow the way I couldn't.

To all of the people who have stuck around through my failures, vulnerabilities, and challenges without judgment and who have become family in the process: you stayed without any sense of duty or need for gratitude, and your selflessness has inspired me to do the same for others – to show up with kindness.

Last but not least, my heartfelt thanks go out to my family. I love you more than I can say. Thank you Saurabh for your patience in listening to all 223 questions at all sorts of odd hours and for your honest feedback. And finally, to my children: you can be anything you want to be – I'm glad you have chosen to be kind.

FOREWORD

I dropped out of college to start my first company when I was 22 years old. Nobody appointed me or promoted me to become the company leader; it just happened organically, as I made our first hire, then the second, then the subsequent ones. Almost without noticing, our company grew to over a hundred members, but unfortunately my leadership and management abilities didn't grow in parallel. I made so many mistakes in that first experience as CEO that I could write a series of books about all the things I messed up.

It's been 16 years now since that first leadership experience, and in that time, I have embarked on a personal journey to become a better leader. This journey has taken me to some of the best business schools in the world, including Kellogg, Harvard, and Stanford. I learned a lot through these programs, but I can honestly share that no leadership class or exercise can compare to the amazing power of self-reflection. It's through self-reflection that I have come to recognize my core values, develop self-compassion, straighten my emotional intelligence, and become more empathetic. All of these have helped me become a better leader and, more importantly, a better person.

What excites me the most about this book is that Devika has combined the best of academic research with years of her own experience as a coach to create a true self-help manual, which provides the roadmap to a profound personal exploration journey that will ultimately make you a more self-aware leader. This is the book I have been looking for throughout the last 16 years of my leadership development journey.

For me, the impact has gone well beyond my own personal exploration. I'm now running my fourth company, and one of the key learnings I have taken away is the importance of every hire for the success of the company. For this reason, even though we are now a team of more than 200 members, I still conduct the final interview of all candidates. Since reading *Reflective Edge: For Senior Executives*, I always include at least one of its question in every interview. It has an almost magical effect. Cultural-fit interviews automatically become candid conversations. Furthermore, besides the interviews, the questions presented in the book have proven to be extremely effective in helping me activate some of the most meaningful conversations I have had with colleagues and friends.

If you are reading this, it means the book has found its way into your hands. Now it is your turn, as Devika says in the book, to find the power to look into yourself – it's where most of your power lies.

Carlos Moncayo
Co-founder and Chief Executive Officer at Inspectorio,
Young Global Leader—World Economic Forum

INTRODUCTION

If you were to write a list of steps you could take to become a more effective and influential leader, which areas would you choose to focus on? Communication? Motivation? What about self-awareness? Would introspection be somewhere on your list?

Research shows that leaders who are self-aware can significantly increase their teams' chances of success. How? By having an awareness of who you are, what has shaped you, and how you respond to the vicissitudes of business and people issues, you can tailor your interactions for maximum effect and influence.

The competitive advantage that comes from understanding your own thoughts, feelings, and behavior patterns is enormous. Not only does it increase self-acceptance, it also increases your acceptance of those around you. The more you know and accept yourself, the more open minded and inclusive you can become. You gain awareness of how you are perceived by others, and you can use this to evolve as you grow in your role.

I have coached many C-suite executives over the years, and when it comes to personal development, I find journaling (asking self-analytical questions) to be one of the most effective tools in my kit.

Common feedback I receive is that self-reflective journaling helps with stress management, mental clarity, and decision making, and the one thing every single client has said is that it has helped them manage people with greater empathy, which in turn has led to an improvement in overall team performance.

It makes perfect sense: once you've acknowledged yourself and had the time to reflect on your own inner stories, you can apply the same considerations to others.

The technique has other applications too. For example, many people find the questions a useful tool for assessing candidates in interview situations, particularly when recruiting senior management – when the stakes are high, attitude becomes one of the most vital criteria for selection. I've also known clients use stories that surfaced from their own journaling as material for inspirational speeches, blogs, and books on leadership. By writing your own stories down, you create the raw material needed to inspire and motivate others.

The CORE components

I approach coaching from a psychoanalytical perspective. As a coach, my primary goal is to help leaders look inward and identify ways to use their learnings to positively influence external interactions.

It's not always easy. Self-reflection can be uncomfortable. Human nature is to seek validation, and our instinct is to try and pass blame and responsibility on to others. But if we can take ownership of our actions, the resilience we gain is unmatchable. Journaling is a reflective process in which you give yourself the privilege of non-judgment. No, it's not easy, but I assure you, it's well worth it.

When working with my clients, I focus on four key pillars: Competence, Ourselves, Reflection and Energy (CORE). 'Competence' is the ability to contribute and serve the world using acquired skills and innate talent. 'Ourselves' is knowing and accepting who we are, including our values, purpose, and even our dark side. 'Reflection' is the act of stepping back in order to observe the situation and the needs of our stakeholders, and 'Energy' relates to how we influence the world with our integrated persona and how we project ourselves through both verbal and non-verbal communication.

By focusing on these pillars and embarking on the journaling process, you will take ownership of your own transformation and bring the 'whole person' into your leadership role. Other benefits include improved confidence and the ability to redefine and rebrand yourself.

Journaling will also help you come to terms with the stories you tend to hold back. As it has done for me, it will help you understand just how far you've come and how you can use your experiences to keep moving forward.

I have journaled for many years, but it wasn't until I wrote a paper about my own life, as part of my training in clinical and organizational psychology at INSEAD, that I understood its true power. To write the paper took a great deal of courage and required me to be honest with myself about who I was and what had shaped me. It is the single most transformational thing I have ever done.

By writing that paper, by looking deep into myself, I realized that I had inner resilience and could break patterns of behavior that didn't serve me anymore. In the years since, I have used journaling to help countless corporate clients with life and career goals, stress, health, influence, confidence, critical thinking, and much more.

There is a cacophony of voices around you telling you who you are. You know amidst all the noise which one is yours. Journaling will enable you to turn the volume of your own voice up while at the same time fading the external noise out.

Questions are key

Each book in the Reflective Edge series contains 223 questions based on the psychoanalytical research of organizations. They draw on several academic studies on the topics of emotional intelligence, influence, self-aware leadership, reflection, and self-worth.

The open-ended questions have all been carefully crafted to offer a counselling-led, motivational, nondirective approach. The idea is for them to provide you with an accessible platform for self-exploration in a noncritical, affirmative way.

This is a true self-help book. Its aim is to provoke and challenge you so that you can discover the answers for your own unique situation. To motivate yourself and evolve as a leader, you need to be evocative. These questions are deeply evocative.

By writing this book and the other books in the series, I hope to share with you some of my coaching practices and expertise so that you can benefit from my professional experience and give yourself the best chance of growing as a leader.

If you want to take things to the next level, I urge you to reach out to a qualified coach with whom you can discuss your answers and who can walk you through the process of transforming your leadership capabilities.

If you would like to reach out to me, please feel free to get in touch via my website – www.COREexecutivepresence.com. I'd be very happy to discuss ways in which we could work together.

How to use this book

When setting out to answer the questions, it's important to come at each one with a clear mindset. If you've spent time mulling them over beforehand, the ideas won't flow naturally. Let each question surprise you. Go in unprepared so that you can tap into your genuine self.

Work through the questions in an order that makes sense for your own personal situation. You may want to start at the front and work from cover to cover (a great option if you want to challenge yourself, as you never know what's coming next), or you may want to flick through to find a question that is pertinent to the 'place' you are in in your career/ life right now.

Grab a journal and a pen, and get writing. When you physically write something out by hand instead of typing, it resonates more deeply. I usually use a fountain pen because I like the flow and also for environmental reasons. Pick good-quality stationary so that it will last for years to come.

It may sound simplistic, but make sure you write down each question and question number for future reference. If you want to add to it later or look back to understand what you were going through at a certain time in your career, it's important to be organized up front.

In terms of how long you should spend on each question, I recommend at least eight minutes of continuous writing. After that, if you feel you would benefit from further unpacking and have the capacity to carry on, keep going.

The silent 'why'

You will notice that most of the questions don't contain the word 'why.' This is because it applies to each and every one, so always keep that one small but hugely important word at the back of your mind when considering your answers.

I recommend following the '5 Whys' technique, which was originally developed by Sakichi Toyoda for the Toyota Motor Corporation. The idea is that you keep asking why, with each answer forming the basis of the next question.

It's a fantastic tool for delving deeper into cause and effect. Keep on asking until you feel you have reached the root cause of the feeling, behavior, or outcome in the context of the original question.

Tips and guidelines to keep in mind

As you work through the book, try to remember the following:

1. **Engage:** This journal should be engaging for you. Allow your outer self (the leader you project) to collaborate with your inner self (the truth of who you are) to create a trusted space in which you can reflect deeply. As you write, allow yourself to let go of any inner resistance towards your goals. Make a 'to-do' list of things that surface. Remember that it is not mandatory to take concrete actions for everything you write. If you use the book purely to gain a better understanding of yourself, it is still time well spent.

2. **Focus:** Stay focused on the process, and remember it will at times be a journey you may not want to go on. It will take discipline and commitment. To make things easier, try to follow your heart, and let it dictate what comes out – grammar, spelling, and handwriting should be the least of your concerns.

3. **Evoke:** Look at your life, and have hope and confidence in your potential. Be honest with yourself – to be an authentic leader, you first need to be genuine in your own company. This journey within will be evocative. It will bring up forgotten memories – some pleasant and some less so. If something crops up that is distressing or too painful to explore, I would suggest waiting before writing about it. Writing will help you heal, but so will time – give yourself a break, and revisit it when you are ready.

4. **Plan:** When you find your authentic voice and want to develop it further, make a commitment to change just one or two things that you feel will make a difference (your engagement style, a limiting belief, etc.). Engage a trusted advisor or thought partner to help you. This could be a coach, counselor, mentor, or transformative leadership program.

Finally, remember that at the core of leadership is our inner world. It's complex, unique, and paradoxical. By journaling, we peek into the myriad of motivators that play out in the vicissitudes of the life of the leader in you.

Looking inward will help, although it will take courage, but then you couldn't have made it this far and achieved so much without having the ability to put yourself forward. Find the courage to look within yourself – it's where most of your power lies. Be true, be present, and take time to know yourself – you deserve it.

Keep this book on your desk. Take it with you when you go away on business or when you think you may have eight minutes to spare before a meeting. It will center your thoughts. Share the book with the other leaders in your organization. As they embark on their own journey of self-reflection, you will notice the power of each person's transformation on the culture and success of your business.

"The most fundamental thing about leadership is to have the humility to continue to get feedback and to try to get better – because your job is to help everybody else get better."

— Jim Yong Kim

THE QUESTIONS

- 1 -

Under extreme pressure, diamonds can be made from anything – even cheese. Crisis can turn us into better people. Which events in your life have taught you about resilience and courage? How are you better off because of them?

I DID IT!

- 2 -

What is your next adventure? What level of self-awareness will you need in order to get the most out of the experience?

- 3 -

How genuine are you with others? What is your truth, and how do you own it? Which aspects of yourself are you afraid to share with the world?

I DID IT!

- 4 -

Traditional leaders led homogenous groups, however, in global leadership, connective leaders are the ones who bring together contradictory groups to create a stronger whole. How are you a connective leader?

I DID IT!

- 5 -

How do you respond to loss? Loss in revenue, loss of a product, loss of an employee, or even a strategic business failure... What does this show about how you grieve? How can you make this process kinder for yourself and for others?

I DID IT!

- 6 -

"I've talked to nearly 30,000 people on this show, and all 30,000 had one thing in common: they all wanted validation," said Oprah. When do you feel most in need of validation? What are the triggers that make you uncomfortable and vulnerable?

I DID IT!

- 7 -

If you met yourself at a business networking

event, why would you like yourself? Would you

want to connect with yourself?

- 8 -

What are your core values? Do the external realities

of your career resonate with your internal values?

How are you living your values every day?

I DID IT!

- 9 -

Change is constant; we are all transitioning into the future self. What makes transition uncomfortable for you, and when do you find it a breeze?

I DID IT!

- 10 -

How do you bring out the intrinsic

goodness in others?

I DID IT!

- 11 -

Fortune favors the bold. When was the last time
you took a risk? Describe the person you were
when you had the conviction to take that risk.
How did you feel?

I DID IT!

- 12 -

Do you use work as a form of escapism? Does it keep you from a passion, a toxic relationship, or from confronting your demons? What are you running away from?

I DID IT!

- 13 -

If you do not participate in mature reflection and evolve as a leader, where will you be in three years? Where are you headed?

I DID IT!

- 14 -

How can you retain a strong sense of who you are while remaining flexible and adaptable at the same time?

I DID IT!

- 15 -

What makes you come alive? Is this aliveness contagious? What do you need to do to bring this sense of aliveness into your workplace? How can you use it to change your team or company culture?

I DID IT!

- 16 -

What conversations were you exposed to while growing up about success and failure? How has this narrative shaped your career choices?

I DID IT!

- 17 -

How have the experiences you didn't get to have

and what you could have become shaped you?

How can you cut your losses and move on?

I DID IT!

- 18 -

Do you have a love of learning? What do you
need to learn and unlearn? What is stopping
you from learning?

I DID IT!

- 19 -

In which aspects of your life do you feel the fear of being irrelevant and unwanted? How much of this fear is unfounded?

I DID IT!

- 20 -

How are the professional learning programs

you have attended in the past serving you now?

What would need an upgrade and why?

I DID IT!

- 21 -

Do you have autonomy in the way that you lead? Who do you think the visible and invisible players influencing this are? How do you pay this forward to your teams? Do they feel trusted with autonomy?

I DID IT!

- 22 -

How do you integrate yourself within your

teams, and how do you differentiate yourself?

Is this a happy balance for you?

I DID IT!

- 23 -

How does the culture of your country of origin influence your style? How do you adapt this to the global working style?

I DID IT!

- 24 -

It is estimated that Wordsworth walked 175,000 miles in his lifetime for inspiration. In all your busyness, how do you step back to search for fresh, creative perspective?

I DID IT!

- 25 -

How do you address an ethical crisis or lack of

integrity within your teams?

I DID IT!

- 26 -

As you hold on to the controls, can you let go a little and enjoy some serendipity from time to time? When was the last time you experienced serendipity?

I DID IT!

- 27 -

Who and what do you take for granted at

your workplace?

I DID IT!

- 28 -

When did you last genuinely thank someone in a way that made them feel acknowledged and celebrated? What are the different ways you do this?

I DID IT!

- 29 -

What is taking up your attention right now? Is it serving your short-term ego needs, or is it serving a long-term greater good?

I DID IT!

- 30 -

How differently would you experience life if you were 10% more open minded? What chances would you take? Who would you include?

I DID IT!

- 31 -

Do you allow time between action and reaction?

How can you stop yourself from using quick-fire

responses to gain instant gratification?

I DID IT!

- 32 -

What gives you absolute joy? Make a go-to list for the times when you could do with some playfulness.

I DID IT!

- 33 -

Who do you have the strongest bonds with, and why?
Have you given them permission (both spoken and
unspoken) to tell you the truth?

I DID IT!

- 34 -

When did you last feel that you were in a constant state of aggression and competitiveness? When this happens, how do you step away from the rat race?

I DID IT!

- 35 -

Who do you compare yourself with? Does this comparison elicit jealousy? What is it that stirs within you to make you feel like this?

I DID IT!

- 36 -

"The grand essentials to happiness in this life are something to do, something to love, and something to hope for," said George Washington Burnap. What are you looking forward to doing in the short term, and why? Who do you love? What are your long-term dreams for yourself?

I DID IT!

- 37 -

What are your goals for yourself in terms of relationships, family, social responsibility, health, and spirituality? How do they fit in with your professional ambitions?

I DID IT!

- 38 -

What is the most grandiose feat you have ever achieved? Which small moments on that journey brought out the best in you?

I DID IT!

- 39 -

At this point in your career, what do you feel your legacy would be? Do you believe that it can be in more than one field? What small steps are you taking to move towards this?

I DID IT!

- 40 -

How often do you put yourself in someone else's shoes? In your last three conversations, did you pause to hear the other person's perspective? How do you know that they are feeling seen and heard?

I DID IT!

- 41 -

Some bridges are meant to be burned. Which ones have

you set fire to? When you grow out of people in your life,

do you judge yourself for moving on?

I DID IT!

- 42 -

Do you feel that you bring your whole self to your workplace? What parts of yourself do you consciously hold back?

I DID IT!

- 43 -

What controls your responses? Is it your inner dialogue, or is it your environment? If both, how much do you listen to each, and how do you decide which one is correct?

I DID IT!

- 44 -

What can you do right now to be happier?

I DID IT!

- 45 -

How much of your current leadership style is spiritual?
What percentage is serenity? When do you come from a
centered place of generosity?

I DID IT!

- 46 -

Why do you think you have skin in the game?

I DID IT!

- 47 -

Does the way you communicate build trust and respect?

What are the three rules you follow to do so?

I DID IT!

- 48 -

What small steps could you take to change the quality of your life? When will you start taking them?

I DID IT!

- 49 -

What would you describe as a successful coaching intervention? How would you like to use the coach as a 'thought partner'?

I DID IT!

- 50 -

Do you believe leaders are born or made? Which leadership traits were you born with, and which ones were made? Was your strongest leadership trait built, or do you feel that you were born with it?

I DID IT!

- 51 -

How do you calm your anxiety, and how do you

manage the anxiety of your teams?

I DID IT!

- 52 -

How do you liberate the potential within yourself?

How can you facilitate this in your teams?

I DID IT!

- 53 -

Can you see through the masks that people wear?

Can you gauge hidden agendas and motivations?

I DID IT!

- 54 -

What are your inner drivers? What intrinsically

fuels your ambition?

I DID IT!

- 55 -

What does being a holistic leader mean to you?

I DID IT!

- 56 -

Can someone benefit from the way you contain your anxiety and manage your vulnerability? What stories can you share to motivate others?

I DID IT!

- 57 -

What makes you believe you are a product of your past?

How do you appreciate the influences of your past in

terms of the person you have become?

I DID IT!

- 58 -

Make a list of adventurous, fearless ideas:
10 books you could write, 10 new initiatives or
ventures, 10 philanthropic plans...

I DID IT!

- 59 -

What are your favorite small-talk stories? What subtle messages on how others should perceive you are you conveying about yourself through these stories?

I DID IT!

- 60 -

Who have you idealized, and why? What is it in them that remains untapped in you? How can you bring this out in yourself?

I DID IT!

- 61 -

Do you try to stay emotionally uninvested in some

assignments in order to feel safe and in control?

What defense processes do you use to distance yourself?

I DID IT!

- 62 -

Have you ever been picked on or bullied at work?

What have these experiences taught you?

I DID IT!

- 63 -

Where in life have you self-sabotaged

your progress, and why?

I DID IT!

- 64 -

Do you have a spiritual practice?

How does it impact your persona?

I DID IT!

- 65 -

Looking back, have you ever scapegoated someone?
Why did you pick them? Is there anything about them
that you are denying within your own self?

I DID IT!

- 66 -

Who do you surround yourself with at work? If your leadership style is a reflection of the five people closest to you, what does this say about you as a leader?

I DID IT!

- 67 -

Have you ever been a minority in a team? Did you feel like a misfit? How has this shaped the way you see diversity and inclusion within your organization?

I DID IT!

- 68 -

What are your narcissistic traits? Would you consider this to be healthy narcissism? How do you check yourself against pathological self-absorption?

I DID IT!

- 69 -

Who would you upset if you were three times more successful than you are now? Is this subtly facilitating any kind of self-sabotage?

I DID IT!

- 70 -

How do you provide vision and strategic direction
to your teams? Is this a democratic conversation?
Is it a fair process?

I DID IT!

- 71 -

Do you get easily bored and thrive on constant

change? How do your teams adapt to this?

What systems and processes help them cope?

I DID IT!

- 72 -

Are you outcome oriented or process oriented,

and why?

I DID IT!

- 73 -

Are you an open book? Which chapters do you keep hidden away?

I DID IT!

- 74 -

Do you have an outlier in your teams? Do you fear dissent, or do you think this person is important for creative, honest conversation?

I DID IT!

- 75 -

Do you enjoy building? What kind of pride do you
feel when you dream and execute? What have you
built recently that you are proud of?

I DID IT!

- 76 -

Do you need to be at the center of achievement and attention? How generously do you share the stage?

I DID IT!

- 77 -

Do you have trouble conforming to structure and organizational rules? What kind of flexibility do you allow yourself?

I DID IT!

- 78 -

Who are the quiet leaders in your teams?

Are they acknowledged?

I DID IT!

- 79 -

Have you ever diminished others at work? If so,

have you forgiven yourself, and how

do you plan to do things differently in the future?

I DID IT!

- 80 -

Can you lead within a variety of cultures?

What international experiences and stories

have left a lifelong impact on you?

I DID IT!

- 81 -

How has each role you have undertaken changed you?

How has this impacted the way you lead in your

current position?

- 82 -

Are you aware that leader-follower relationships are reflective of parent-child relationships? How does this parentalized leadership dynamic serve you?

I DID IT!

- 83 -

There are enough diamonds in the world to give everyone on the planet a cupful, yet everyone considers them to be precious. How do you make yourself stand out so that others feel privileged to have your time and attention?

I DID IT!

- 84 -

How do you add to the collective pride of your teams?

I DID IT!

- 85 -

Can you adapt your style to lead virtual teams? Can you motivate and communicate effectively, offering feedback and encouragement via technology? Does the nature of your primary task change when you lead virtual teams?

I DID IT!

- 86 -

According to research, 89% of success depends
on your presence. Do you feel you have
leadership presence? Why?

I DID IT!

- 87 -

What associations come to mind when you hear the phrase 'top dog'? Are you one? Who do you think is, and why?

I DID IT!

- 88 -

Do you have a personal development plan? What three
aspects of yourself would you like to work on?

I DID IT!

- 89 -

Are you aware that cognitive arguments alone are not enough when trying to change how people perceive a situation? Do you use an evocative approach as well? Do you adapt this approach to your audience's needs?

I DID IT!

- 90 -

How are you building a community and tribe?
Standing on the outside looking in, what do think
the tribe stands for?

I DID IT!

- 91 -

Are you living a life of unrealized potential
because you fear the attention and judgement of
your loved ones and peers?

I DID IT!

- 92 -

What have been your most personal defining moments?

I DID IT!

- 93 -

When have you felt you were serving a cause greater than yourself? Describe that feeling.

I DID IT!

- 94 -

When were you last full of confusion, distractions, and feelings of setback? Did you know these moments were building you for something greater? What breakthrough moments have you gone through that were also moments of possible breakdown?

I DID IT!

- 95 -

What has to happen in the next three years for you
to feel that the years leading up to that point have
been successful?

I DID IT!

- 96 -

How much does money motivate you? If it does,
what caused you to feel that success is about acquiring
more things?

I DID IT!

- 97 -

Do you have the persistence and patience to lead change?
Where are you anticipating resistance? Do you have the
courage to be disliked?

I DID IT!

- 98 -

What you should celebrate about your life?

I DID IT!

- 99 -

Were you aware and centered today? What was the quality of your awareness on a scale of one to 10?

I DID IT!

- 100 -

What personal systems and processes would you change

in order to be more productive?

I DID IT!

- 101 -

Do you take time to maintain interaction, contact, and engagement in personal relationships, such as with your close friends, partner, kids, parents, etc.? Write down three novel, creative ways you can do this in the next three months.

I DID IT!

- 102 -

Good things in life are free. What are the simple, good things in your life that are absolutely free? How are you spreading this goodness?

I DID IT!

- 103 -

How do you vent anger? What assumptions do you

make when you are angry?

- 104 -

Do you think you have exceeded or fulfilled the expectations of your family of origin? How were these expectations communicated to you?

I DID IT!

- 105 -

When you enter a room, are you switched on enough to observe the dynamics at play? How has this helped you in the past?

I DID IT!

- 106 -

Why should anyone be led by you? What's in it

for them?

I DID IT!

- 107 -

In a crisis, people pay attention, which may put you center stage. What is your secret to being 'graceful under fire'?

I DID IT!

- 108 -

What will be your unique contribution to the world?

I DID IT!

- 109 -

What are your superpowers as a leader? If you were
granted three more superpowers, what would you
want them to be?

I DID IT!

- 110 -

How do you get your buy-ins? Is there something different you could do?

I DID IT!

- 111 -

Have you ever withheld information? What rules of

transparency do you follow?

I DID IT!

- 112 -

Who listens to your life plans intently? Who gives you the safe space needed to connect with what is emerging from within?

I DID IT!

- 113 -

What different areas of expertise do you have? What does this say about the breadth of your interests?

I DID IT!

- 114 -

How quickly can you take diverse information from a variety of sources and make it applicable to you? When do you anticipate to do that next?

I DID IT!

- 115 -

"The challenge of using simple language is you have to know what you are talking about." — *The New York Times*. Do you or does anyone in your teams hide behind jargon? How do you keep communication succinct?

I DID IT!

- 116 -

Do you command respect from your seniors? What small steps do you need to take to build your credibility?

I DID IT!

- 117 -

Do you motivate your teams to make decisions and take ownership without you? Are they validated for having the courage to be self-leaders? If so, what concrete actions have you taken to show your appreciation for this?

I DID IT!

- 118 -

How long does it take for you to understand a new team member's work style? Do you work well with those who have a completely different style to you?

I DID IT!

- 119 -

Are you participating in your life as a whole

human being?

I DID IT!

- 120 -

Do you have a tendency to procrastinate complex problems, or do you make decisions quickly? What are you trying to protect within yourself by procrastinating?

I DID IT!

- 121 -

How have your social relationships contributed to your sense of self, and how have they influenced you in terms of wanting to build your reputation?

I DID IT!

- 122 -

What changes is your organization going through?

How are you contributing toward a stronger

organizational capability?

I DID IT!

- 123 -

What rules of leadership do you follow? Are there

any caveats?

I DID IT!

- 124 -

When were you last in a state of deeply sensing your environment? How does centered listening from your third eye and third ear give you an advantage?

I DID IT!

- 125 -

Do you assume that others share your view? When have you had conflict around ideologies? How did you feel, and how was the conflict managed?

I DID IT!

- 126 -

What are the triggers that rile you up emotionally? What is the source of these triggers? Are they unfounded fears, or are they actually relevant to the life that you lead?

I DID IT!

- 127 -

If you could be 10% kinder at work, how would people's perception of you change? How would the energy within your teams change?

I DID IT!

- 128 -

Does your personal leadership style have room to evolve?
How do you decide what to learn and unlearn in order to
enable your evolution?

I DID IT!

- 129 -

Have you ever had to make use of limited information and resources to move ahead with a task? When was the last time you were able to pull off a task like this successfully? What lessons did you learn?

I DID IT!

- 130 -

Passion is contagious. What is it about your profession that makes your heart sing?

I DID IT!

- 131 -

What three stories can you share that have shaped

you as a thought leader?

I DID IT!

- 132 -

Where are you controlling too much, and

where do you need to let go?

I DID IT!

- 133 -

How long is long enough in your current role? When do you plan to challenge the confines of your position and reinvent yourself?

I DID IT!

- 134 -

Does your personal sense of identity stem from your actions? Are you an 'I-ACT-therefore-I-AM' type of leader? When do you step back and surrender to the process?

I DID IT!

- 135 -

What is your digital presence like? If you were to position yourself as a thought leader, what ideas do you have that are worth sharing? Which digital platforms would you use to increase visibility, and how would you use them?

I DID IT!

- 136 -

How do you bring more playfulness to your organization? Whose idea of playfulness do you indulge in? Yours or others?

I DID IT!

- 137 -

Sometimes you need to get on the balcony and distance yourself from the action in order to gain perspective and see what is really happening. How often do you get on the balcony? Have you seen anything interesting lately?

I DID IT!

- 138 -

Do your teams use a shared language to minimize misunderstandings? Do you adapt your vocabulary in order to connect and set standards for a common lingo?

I DID IT!

- 139 -

When emotions take center stage in teams,

how do you lead?

I DID IT!

- 140 -

What does it mean for you to thrive professionally?
Who are the beneficiaries of this thriving leader that
emerges from within you?

I DID IT!

- 141 -

What do you do to preserve your organization's heritage? How do you incorporate previous wisdom into progressive adaptations?

I DID IT!

- 142 -

What, according to you, is the difference between leadership and authority? Where do you use leadership and where do you use authority in your role, and why?

I DID IT!

- 143 -

True maturity makes you comfortable with the unknown. Are you truly mature, and how can you make yourself comfortable with the unpredictability and ambiguity of life?

I DID IT!

- 144 -

They say progress is often accompanied by distress.

Where in your life are you going through deep change?

Are you showing compassion to yourself and others

affected by this?

I DID IT!

- 145 -

What stories do you use to articulate your values

and purpose?

I DID IT!

- 146 -

Do you sometimes micromanage just to be a
self-righteous martyr? Who has to give up their autonomy
and ownership of a task in order for you to do this?

I DID IT!

- 147 -

Do your teams clearly understand the common vision, aspirations, values, and mission that bind them together? How does this help them to collaborate productively?

I DID IT!

- 148 -

What new ideas are you experimenting with in your
organization? Who is in your core creative team?
What small, adaptive changes are you making?

I DID IT!

- 149 -

Can you have an honest, courageous conversation with yourself and name the elephant in the room? Are you making your teams feel safe enough so that they can name the elephant too?

I DID IT!

- 150 -

What is the extent of your leadership influence?

Do you share your ideas and insights across

boundaries and functions?

I DID IT!

- 151 -

Do you feel that you have 'arrived' yet?

What are the signs?

I DID IT!

- 152 -

When was the last time you unexpectedly celebrated someone else's achievement? How was it giving the entire spotlight without agenda to another person?

I DID IT!

- 153 -

Do you bring a network advantage to your organization?

How did you build it, and how can you increase its scope?

I DID IT!

- 154 -

What do you fear about working with alien cultures?
When have you felt like a misfit? What does this say
about how you use your courage to connect?

I DID IT!

- 155 -

In which areas of your life are small changes happening? Where are you surrendering to the outcome, and where are you leading with purpose?

I DID IT!

- 156 -

Do you give before you take? Where do you give more than you take and vice versa?

I DID IT!

- 157 -

The Japanese have 16 ways of saying no, yet none of them can be directly translated into "no." How many ways do you use to say no? When did you last say it? Was it compassionate, kind, and firm?

I DID IT!

- 158 -

As you adapt to change, are you open to
redefining what success means? Are you making
serendipitous discoveries?

I DID IT!

- 159 -

Do you have global leadership skills? Do you hire people with global competence in order to have a competitive edge? Has this decision paid off?

I DID IT!

- 160 -

If there was one consistent message you would like to communicate to your audience, what would it be, and why?

I DID IT!

- 161 -

Do you simplify or complicate life?

Why do you feel this is?

I DID IT!

- 162 -

There are two modes of change: short term and long term. Which one are you committed to?

I DID IT!

- 163 -

Do people bring their problems to managers in your teams? Are you approachable, and do you lead by example to keep lines of communication open? In which instances have you felt approachable?

I DID IT!

- 164 -

Do you feel the need to be the 'hero' in times of crisis?

Do you feel your personal success has been a hero's journey?

I DID IT!

- 165 -

Have you faced xenophobia, ethnocentricity or nationalism in your global career? What has this taught you about inclusive leadership?

I DID IT!

- 166 -

Did you know that setting difficult goals increases effort and consequently enhances performance? What difficult goals have you set for yourself?

I DID IT!

- 167 -

Before you say or do something that involves others, do you engage with them? Do you use fair processes when decision making?

I DID IT!

- 168 -

What makes you feel uncomfortable and defensive?

Is your response rational, or is it driven by emotions?

I DID IT!

Do you have a fear of being excluded? If so, how does this present itself? Can you seem distant and aloof at times? How do you deal with collaborative anxiety?

I DID IT!

- 170 -

In multiparty negotiations, do you understand ego

dynamics, assumptions, and hidden agendas?

I DID IT!

- 171 -

What do you feel about asking for help, admitting an error, or being the voice of dissent?

I DID IT!

- 172 -

Who you have become, and who are you becoming?

To what extent is this in your hands?

I DID IT!

- 173 -

Parrhesia is the ability to speak the truth. Do you have the courage to speak truth to yourself?

I DID IT!

- 174 -

Do you often step back to pay attention to the collective emotions of specific stakeholders, such as board members, investors, suppliers, employers, or unions?

I DID IT!

- 175 -

How do you decipher rational and irrational fears in others? What would be the consequences of not having the skill to do so in your role?

- 176 -

Do you feel a loss of individuality when you are in a large group? How do you deal with that loss of identity?

I DID IT!

- 177 -

How do you maneuver the blame game in a crisis?

I DID IT!

- 178 -

What are your non-negotiable boundaries?
Which events have taught you the importance of
boundaries in relationships?

I DID IT!

- 179 -

The term valency in chemistry refers to inherent characteristics of a substance that are activated by being exposed to external conditions. Has an external situation brought out a surprisingly inherent characteristic in you? How was it being 'out of character' and surprising yourself?

I DID IT!

- 180 -

When creating a new team, do you observe how the group naturally organizes itself, or do you set the tone of communication as well as the task and structure?

I DID IT!

- 181 -

Are your teams gender inclusive? What factors do you think this choice is built on? How would your organization be impacted by more diversity?

I DID IT!

- 182 -

What life lessons did you learn outside the classroom when growing up? Do memories of these moments spark joy or discomfort?

I DID IT!

- 183 -

When were you last in transition? Was this time fraught with mixed feelings as you let go of past identities and welcomed in a new one?

I DID IT!

- 184 -

What is your vision of the ideal future you?

What are the possibilities? Can you list them

without limiting yourself?

I DID IT!

- 185 -

Is there resistance to women's leadership within your industry and organization? If there are successful women in your teams, what silent trade-offs do you think they are making for their careers?

I DID IT!

- 186 -

Are you a transformational or a transactional leader?

What would your followers say?

I DID IT!

- 187 -

What have the demands of your family life taught

you about being an empathetic leader?

I DID IT!

- 188 -

When individuals in your teams are going through periods of deep transition, do you seek opportunities to engage with them so that they don't interpret your distance as you being unapproachable?

I DID IT!

- 189 -

The higher you are in the organization, the more quickly
you will transition through change. This is because
you have the vantage point of seeing the destination
clearly. How do you communicate this change to your
subordinates in order to ease the transition for them?

I DID IT!

- 190 -

Even cows moo in different accents. How do you include others in your conversations, especially in global situations, where culture and language may differ?

I DID IT!

What do you think you encourage more: active membership or passive manipulators? What would you do differently?

- 192 -

People follow people who they look up to and are proud to be associated with. Do others feel pride at being associated with you?

I DID IT!

- 193 -

What processes do you follow to identify and discuss potential crises and hidden opportunities within those crises? Who is part of this conversation, and what is the quality of their contribution?

I DID IT!

- 194 -

How do you encourage nontraditional ideas, activities, and actions in order to bring in newer perspectives?

I DID IT!

- 195 -

In your experience, does leadership development

and succession planning empower team leaders?

- 196 -

Can you communicate your vision in less than three minutes and get a response of understanding and interest? What would you say? How would you adapt the message for your audience?

I DID IT!

- 197 -

Where have you earmarked short-term wins to help maintain high levels of urgency and accountability?

I DID IT!

- 198 -

Money is not always a motivator, yet it is always an expensive one. Small and unexpected methods of acknowledgement have huge effects on motivation. What small things can you do to motivate your teams?

I DID IT!

- 199 -

Malcom Gladwell's 'law of the few' suggests that rare and connected people shape the world. He defined three types of influential people: mavens (discerning people who accumulate knowledge and share advice), connectors (who know lots of people), and salespeople (who have the natural ability to influence and persuade others). Which one are you, and why?

I DID IT!

- 200 -

What is your aspirational leadership style? Who do you know with this style, and can you use them as a role model to be inspired by and emulate?

I DID IT!

- 201 -

How often do you remind others and yourself about past failures? Does this make you and others feel diminished and risk averse?

I DID IT!

- 202 -

Are you connected to the realities of your business at ground level? When did you last roll up your sleeves? How do you use this to strategize?

I DID IT!

- 203 -

The strong connection your subordinates have

with you may impede your analysis of your own

leadership style. How do you get to the objective

truth about how you lead?

I DID IT!

- 204 -

Pride and dignity are important feelings. What brings you both pride and dignity in your profession?

I DID IT!

- 205 -

Who are or were the humblest people in your life?

What have you learned from them about how to

treat others?

I DID IT!

- 206 -

What three events have changed the trajectory of your life? Were some of them difficult? Are you grateful for them now?

I DID IT!

- 207 -

Stalin had shamans thrown out of helicopters to give them a chance to prove they could fly. What are your thoughts on overcommitting and underdelivering for yourself and others?

I DID IT!

- 208 -

What words of advice from a mentor have helped you in

your achievements so far?

I DID IT!

- 209 -

Clarity can come from acknowledging that you don't know something. What is it that you don't know?

I DID IT!

- 210 -

What, according to you, makes a moment truly decisive?

I DID IT!

- 211 -

My cat can run faster than Usain Bolt. Do you use the same yardstick to measure the performance of each of your team members?

I DID IT!

- 212 -

How do you identify opportunity when you and your

teams are going through reputational crisis?

I DID IT!

- 213 -

What is seeking to manifest through you?

I DID IT!

- 214 -

Do the values communicated by your organization give you direction and guidance, or are they just slogans on a wall?

I DID IT!

- 215 -

Do you exude both competence and warmth?

How do they show up in your interactions?

I DID IT!

- 216 -

They say that happiness is like a butterfly – it may gently land on you if you are still. When are you still?

I DID IT!

- 217 -

Oranges are berries and strawberries aren't. When was the last time you looked at something mundane in a different light? Should you be doing that more often?

I DID IT!

- 218 -

When did you last blow your socks off?

What happened?

I DID IT!

- 219 -

More than 50% of NASA employees are dyslexic,
hired for their superior spatial awareness skills.
What are the nonobvious skills that you look for in
your hires?

I DID IT!

- 220 -

All the books ever written in English use words comprising 26 letters. Everything complicated is broken down into simple parts. How does simplicity show up in the way you build processes?

I DID IT!

- 221 -

Everyone has a dark side. What is the dark side of leadership within you? How do you manage it?

I DID IT!

- 222 -

The guillotine weighed more than 175 pounds and was dropped from a height of 14 feet. If you could get rid of one person in your office, whose head would roll?

I DID IT!

- 223 -

On April 18, 1930, the BBC announced that there was "no news today." How do prevent your teams from being overwhelmed by information overload? What are your 'need-to-know' policies?

I DID IT!

REFERENCES

1. Avolio, B. J., Walumbwa, F. O. & Weber, T. J. (2009). Leadership: Current Theories, Research, and Future Directions. *Annual Review of Psychology, Vol. 60,* 421–429.

2. Cameron, K. S. (2008). A Process for Changing Organizational Culture. *Handbook of Organizational Development,* 429–445.

3. Chapman, J. & Long, S. D. (2009). Role contamination: is the poison in the person or in the bottle? *Organizations and People: Toxic Leadership, Vol. 15*(3), 40–48.

4. Conger, J. A. (1989). *The Charismatic Leader: Behind the Mystique of Exceptional Leadership.* Jossey-Bass.

5. Eberly, M. B., Johnson, M. D., Hernandez, M. & Avolio B. J. (2013). An integrative process model of leadership: examining loci, mechanics, and event cycles. *American Psychologist, Vol. 68*(6), 427–443.

6. Eisenbeiss, S. A. (2012). Re-thinking ethical leadership: An interdisciplinary integrative approach. *The Leadership Quarterly, Vol. 23*(5), 791–808.

7. Fyke, J. P. & Buzzanel, P. M. (2013). The ethics of conscious capitalism: Wicked problems in leading change and changing leaders. *Human Relations, Vol. 66*(12), 1619–1643.

8.   George, J. M. (2000). Emotions and leadership: The role of emotional intelligence. *Human Relations, Vol. 53* (8), 1027–1055.

9.   Goffee, R. & Jones, G. (2000). Why Should Anyone Be Led by You? *Harvard Business Review*, September–October.

10.   Harakas, P. (2013). Resistance, motivational interviewing, and executive coaching. *Consulting Psychology Journal: Practice and Research, Vol. 65* (2), 108–127.

11.   Heifetz, R., Grashow, A. & Linsky, M. (2009). *The Theory Behind the Practice: A Brief Introduction to the Adaptive Leadership Framework*. Harvard Business Press.

12.   Hirschhorn, L. & Gilmore, T. (1992). The New Boundaries of the "Boundaryless" Company. *Harvard Business Review*, May–June.

13.   Huy, Q. N. (1999). Emotional Capability, Emotional Intelligence, and Radical Change. *The Academy of Management Review, Vol. 24* (2), 325–345.

14.   Jones, H. B. (2001). Magic, Meaning and Leadership: Weber's Model and the Empirical Literature. *Human Relations, Vol. 54* (6), 753–771.

15. Kets de Vries, M. F. R. (2008). Decoding the Team Conundrum: The Eight Roles Executives Play. *Organizational Dynamics, Vol. 36* (1), 28–44.

16. Kets de Vries, M. F. R. (1999). High-Performance Teams: Lessons from the Pygmies. *Organizational Dynamics, Vol. 27* (3), 66–77.

17. Kets de Vries, M. F. R. (1989). *Prisoners of Leadership*. Wiley.

18. Kets de Vries, M. F. R. (2014). The Psycho-path to Disaster: Coping with SOB Executives. *Organizational Dynamics, Vol. 43* (1), 17–26.

19. Kets de Vries, M. F. R. (2006). The Spirit of Despotism: Understanding the Tyrant Within. *Human relations, Vol. 59* (2). 195–220.

20. Kotter, J. P. (2007). Leading Change: Why transformation Efforts Fail. *Harvard Business Review*, January.

21. Levinson, H. (2002). *Organizational Assessment: A Step-by-Step Guide to Effective Consulting*. American Psychological Association.

22. Long, S. (2008). *The Perverse Organization and its Deadly Sins*. Karnac Books.

23.   Maccoby, M. (2004). Why People Follow the Leader: The Power of Transference. *Harvard Business Review*, September.

24.   Morris, J. A., Brotheridge, C. M. & Urbanski, J. C. (2005). Bringing humility to leadership: Antecedents and consequences of leader humility. *Human Relations, Vol. 58*(10), 1323–1350.

25.   Obholzer, A. (1996). Psychoanalytic contributions to authority and leadership issues. *Leadership & Organization Development Journal, Vol. 17*(6), 53–56.

26.   O'Reilly, C. A. & Chatman, J. A. (1996). Culture as social control: Corporations, cults, and commitment. *Research in Organizational Behavior, Vol. 18*, 157–200.

27.   Rokeach, M., & Cochkane, R. (1972). Self-Confrontation and Confrontation With Another as Determinants of Long-Term Value Change. *Journal of Applied Social Psychology, Vol. 2*(4), 283–292.

28.   Sorcher, M. & Brant, J. (2002). Are You Picking the Right Leaders? *Harvard Business Review*, February.

29.   van Ginkel, W., Tindale, R. S. & van Knippenberg, D. (2009). Team reflexivity, development of shared task representations, and the use of distributed information in group decision making. *Group Dynamics: Theory, Research, and Practice, Vol. 13*(4), 265–280.

30. Ward, G., van de Loo, E. & ten Have. S. (2014). Psychodynamic Group Coaching: A Literature Review. *International Journal of Evidence Based Coaching and Mentoring, Vol 12*(1), 63–78.

31. Westra, H. A. & Aviram, A. (2013). Core Skills in Motivational Interviewing. *Psychotherapy, Vol. 50*(3), 273–278.

32. Zaleznik, A. (1997). Real Work, *Harvard Business Review*, November–December.

SUGGESTED READING

1. *Dare to Lead: Brave Work. Tough Conversations. Whole Hearts*, Brené Brown

2. *Mindset: The New Psychology of Success*, Carol S. Dweck

3. *Principles: Life and Work*, Ray Dalio

4. *Purpose, Incorporated: Turning Cause Into Your Competitive Advantage*, John Wood & Amalia McGibbon

5. *Talking to Strangers: What We Should Know About the People We Don't Know*, Malcolm Gladwell

6. *The Leadership Mystique: Leading Behavior in the Human Enterprise*, Manfred Kets de Vries

7. *The Myth of the Strong Leader: Political Leadership in the Modern Age*, Archie Brown

8. *Theory U: Learning from the Future as It Emerges*, C. Otto Scharmar

9. *Working Identity: Unconventional Strategies for Reinventing Your Career*, Herminia Ibarra

ABOUT THE AUTHOR

Devika Das is a speaker, trainer, and C-suite coach who specializes in leadership transformation. The founder of the CORE* method of executive presence training (Competence, Ourselves, Reflection and Energy), Devika uses the principles of psychology to enhance the professional influence of senior leaders.

With an international career spanning over 25 years, Devika has worked across the Middle East and Asia-Pacific, including 10 years working in mainland China. Her clients include senior executives from a wide range organizations and industries, including retail, banking, law, media, and infrastructure.

Using a series of unique training tools, which she developed to help take coaching conversations from mere transactions to transformational interactions, Devika typically works with her clients in small groups or one-on-one settings and assures confidentiality to all her coaching clients.

Devika's specialist areas include:

- Identifying and transforming dysfunctional leadership styles to create impactful executive presence.
- Nurturing personal leadership styles, helping executives develop an adaptable and authentic signature voice as well as values, purpose and legacy.
- Leading with 'night vision,' coaching on how to read power dynamics.

As a graduate of INSEAD's Executive Masters in Clinical and Organizational Psychology (EMCCC), Devika's interests are interpersonal perspective, leadership dynamics within groups and teams, and organizational change from both a micro and macro stand.

Devika is a member of the International Society for the Psychoanalytic Study of Organizations (ISPSO).

---

*Discover how CORE can help transform your leadership style at www.COREexecutivepresence.com.

Made in the USA
Middletown, DE
22 October 2020

21847413R00151